L

Abhijit Naskar is the twenty-first century Neuroscientist whose contributions in Cognitive and Behavioral Neuroscience have helped the world tackle the issues of systemic racism, prejudice, hate, extremism, discrimination and biases more effectively. As an untiring advocate of mental health and universal acceptance, he became a beloved best-selling author all over the world with his very first book "The Art of Neuroscience in Everything". With his pioneering ventures into the Neuropsychology of beliefs and biases, he has hugely contributed in the eradication of religious and cultural differences in our world, for which he is popularly hailed as the humanitarian scientist, who takes the human civilization in the path of sweet general harmony.

GENTE MENTE
ADELANTE

Prejudice Conquered is
World Conquered

ABHIJIT NASKAR

Gente Mente Adelante:

Prejudice Conquered is World Conquered

Copyright © 2021 Abhijit Naskar

This is a work of non-fiction

An Amazon Publishing Company, 1st Edition, 2021

Printed in the United States of America

ISBN: 9798545271252

Also by Abhijit Naskar

The Art of Neuroscience in Everything
Your Own Neuron: A Tour of Your Psychic Brain
The God Parasite: Revelation of Neuroscience
The Spirituality Engine
Love Sutra: The Neuroscientific Manual of Love
Homo: A Brief History of Consciousness
Neurosutra: The Abhijit Naskar Collection
Autobiography of God: Biopsy of A Cognitive Reality
Biopsy of Religions: Neuroanalysis towards Universal
Tolerance
Prescription: Treating India's Soul
What is Mind?
In Search of Divinity: Journey to The Kingdom of Conscience
Love, God & Neurons: Memoir of a scientist who found
himself by getting lost
The Islamophobic Civilization: Voyage of Acceptance
Neurons of Jesus: Mind of A Teacher, Spouse & Thinker
Neurons, Oxygen & Nanak
The Education Decree
Principia Humanitas
The Krishna Cancer
Rowdy Buddha: The First Sapiens
We Are All Black: A Treatise on Racism
The Bengal Tigress: A Treatise on Gender Equality
Either Civilized or Phobic: A Treatise on Homosexuality
Wise Mating: A Treatise on Monogamy
Illusion of Religion: A Treatise on Religious
Fundamentalism
The Film Testament
Human Making is Our Mission: A Treatise on Parenting
I Am The Thread: My Mission
7 Billion Gods: Humans Above All
Lord is My Sheep: Gospel of Human
Morality Absolute
A Push in Perception
Let The Poor Be Your God
Conscience over Nonsense
Saint of The Sapiens
Time to Save Medicine
Fabric of Humanity
Build Bridges not Walls: In the name of Americana
The Constitution of The United Peoples of Earth

Lives to Serve Before I Sleep
When Humans Unite: Making A World Without Borders
All For Acceptance
Monk Meets World
Mission Reality
Citizens of Peace: Beyond The Savagery of Sovereignty
Operation Justice: To Make A Society That Needs No Law
See No Gender
The Gospel of Technology
Every Generation Needs Caretakers: The Gospel of
Patriotism
Aşkanjali: The Sufi Sermon
Mad About Humans: World Maker's Almanac
Revolution Indomable
When Call The People: My World My Responsibility
No Foreigner Only Family
Hurricane Humans: Give me accountability, I'll give you
peace
Ain't Enough to Look Human
Servitude is Sanctitude
Time To End Democracy: The Meritocratic Manifesto
I Vicdansaadet Speaking: No Rest Till The World is Lifted
Boldly Comes Justice: Sentient not Silent
Good Scientist: When Science and Service Combine
Sleepless for Society
Neden Türk: The Gospel of Secularism
Martyr Meets World: To Solve The Hard Problem of
Inhumanity
The Shape of A Human: Our America Their America
When Veins Ignite: Either Integration or Degradation
Heart Force One: Need No Gun to Defend Society
Solo Standing on Guard: Life Before Law
Generation Corazon: Nationalism is Terrorism
Mucize Insan: When The World is Family
Hometown Human: To Live For Soil and Society
Girl Over God: The Novel

DEDICATION

*This book is dedicated to the reformers
who'll come after me.*

Don't just swallow my ideas, expand!

CONTENTS

1. Forward Ever, Backward Never

Gente mente adelante, no retrocedas oh valiente - that is - Forward O People, Forward O Mind, no matter the pangs, never look behind! By looking behind, I don't mean to look, rather I mean to fall behind. And how do we fall behind - not just as individuals, but also as a society? We fall behind when we deny growth - when we assume perfection and deny correction - when we hold on to our tradition so hard that tradition becomes more valuable to us than life itself.

And let me make one thing very clear. I've got no beef with tradition, but I ain't gonna let no tradition triumph over society at the expense of humanity. Forward ever, backward never. Remember, the struggle isn't over till the last oppressed community becomes equal. The struggle isn't over till the last drop of tear is wiped out.

This is not my belief, this is the fundamental principle of societal development - a fact of humanity. You see, I don't have beliefs, I have convictions, absolutely incorruptible, uncompromisable convictions - convictions for which I will not kill anyone, but for which I will happily die myself.

Now, I beg you not to philosophize or intellectualize this with terms like woke or activism, for this is no such thing, this is just plain humanity. Drinking water to hydrate yourself is not hydrationism, it's just life, likewise - standing up to the inhumanities of society is not activism, it's just humanity.

This struggle against inhumanity is the most sacred of all struggles. And as I said, the struggle isn't over till the last oppressed community turns equal - the struggle isn't over till every person on earth feels at home. Equality is not luxury, it's necessity. It is a fundamental requirement of civilization.

Equality facilitates harmony, and harmony further facilitates equality. But mark you, I am not talking about simply believing in harmony, for harmony is no belief. I don't believe in harmony, for if I did, it'd be like saying, I believe in water. There is no life without water, likewise there's no humanity without harmony. It's not a belief, it's a fact of life.

Equality, harmony, diversity - these are not something you believe, these are the foundation of a civilized lifeform, hence, these are life itself.

Or to put it absolutely plainly, there is no nationality, religion, race or gender, there's only humanity.

2. Sonnet of Fundamentals

Sonnet of Fundamentals

Equality, harmony, diversity,
These are not something you believe.
Just like water, air and food,
These are not something you believe.
Fundamentals of human life,
Are beyond all pettiness of opinion.
Argumentation may have its place,
But we must distinguish facts from fiction.
Plenty are the minds so are the beliefs,
But beliefs mustn't undermine humanity.
All of us are dumb, some less some more,
So we must place people before rigidity.
No belief is ultimate, no opinion olympian.
Putting aside truth, let us first be human.

3. Ever Onward to Equality
   (The Sonnet)

Ever Onward to Equality*
(The Sonnet)

Someone once said,
Ever onward to victory.
I say to you today,
Ever onward to equality.
Though the objective is the same,
In path lies the distinction.
I'll say it plainly, to live is to grow,
Including the means of revolution.
Liberty is fundamental in life,
But not by harming the innocent.
Revolution of arms is revolution no more,
What's needed is revolution in conscience.
So I say, let us sacrifice all for society.
Let us rise as soldiers of universal amity.

*I wrote this sonnet originally in Spanish, entitled
"Hasta La Igualdad Siempre", then rewrote in English.

4. Hasta La Igualdad Simpre
(El Soneto)

Hasta La Igualdad Siempre
(El Soneto)

Alguien dijo una vez,
Hasta la victoria siempre.
Pero te digo hoy,
Hasta la igualdad siempre.
El objetivo puede ser el mismo,
Pero los caminos no son los mismos.
Yo digo hoy, vivir es crecer,
Incluso la definición de revolución.
La libertad es fundamental,
Pero no lastimar al inocente.
Las armas no son revolución,
Es una conciencia incorruptible.
Sacrifiquemos todo por la sociedad.
Seamos soldados de la unidad.

5. Into The Void of Realization

ABHIJIT NASKAR

Philosophizing the elements of life may make you feel intellectual, but they don't empower those elements one bit, either in your own life or in society. So pay attention to life, not to words - not to intellectual terminologies.

Study all the philosophies in the world if you so desire, but never take the words to be the ideas. The words are not the idea, they are only a means of comprehension, not of realization. To realize an idea you must go beyond the words.

You see, realization has no words, it's a highly potent void, which gives birth to all the ideas and words in the world. And this void cannot be chained with concepts of narrowness, such as nationality, religion, gender and so on – not even with apparently mystical terms such as spirituality, metaphysics and so on.

Discard all narrowness, discard all walls, discard all sects and dive into the infinite void of realization inside your mind and you'll discover priceless jewels of illumination, then bring those jewels up to the surface and put them to use in the fulfillment of your life's purpose - of your life's work.

Grow so big with your work that your nationality becomes meaningless. Grow so big with your work that you become a national hero of every nation. The heroes of humanity don't call themselves hero in front of others, but in their heart they say, "if I can't be a national hero for every nation, I'd rather not be one". Such is the vastness of a heroic heart.

The hero doesn't say, 'look at me, I am a hero' - the hero says to those who have no strength, 'come my friend, hold my hand, let us rise together.' These are the heroes of humanity - these are the lifters of society, the makers of civilization - these are the true messengers of peace – these are the actual torchbearers of progress.

These are the strongest people on earth, but at the same time, they are the calmest people on earth. They are strong because they are calm, for calm is not weakness, calm is the sign of strength overcoming weakness.

6. Crazy Not Callous
    (The Sonnet)

Crazy Not Callous*
(The Sonnet)

I'm crazy,
But not obnoxious.
I'm free in mind,
But not callous.
I'm ignorant in many things,
But I ain't no intolerant.
I may not know much etiquette,
I know caring with commitment.
I am but a lover most naïve,
No scholar of nothin'.
I am but a warrior unbending,
Got no time for philosophizin'.
To live for people is the mission.
In lifting the fallen lies salvation.

*I wrote this sonnet originally in Spanish, entitled
"Loco, No Irresponsable", then rewrote in English.

7. Loco, No Irresponsable
(El Soneto)

Loco, No Irresponsable
(El Soneto)

Estoy loco,
Pero no indifferente.
Estoy libre,
Pero no irresponsable.
Puedo ser ignorante,
Pero no intolerante.
No sé la etiqueta,
Pero sé cómo amarte.
Soy un amante,
No un erudito.
Soy un guerrero,
No un filósofo.
Vivir para la gente,
Es la misión de mi mente.

8. No Guns, Period

All my life I have spoken of peace and integration, but don't confuse my calm to be my weakness, for when the day comes for me to defend those I care about, I cannot guarantee the safety of the person I have to defend against. Actually I can, but you get my drift. And this is where I must bring up the necessity of the capacity of self-defense, which I haven't done before in detail.

I have emphasized only on the strength of character so far in all my works, but now I'm compelled to emphasized on physical agility as well, particularly because a new threat looms over our world, the threat of White Terrorism. And though I desperately hope that you and your family may never have to face it, if you do, you must be mentally and physically prepared to stand as shield without firearms against such inhuman elements to defend your loved ones.

But again, I repeat - no guns, period. Concerned about self-defense? Learn Martial Arts. Martial arts is not about fighting, it is about being fit and healthy, both physiologically and psychologically. I don't train so I could fight, I train so I could restrain someone from fighting.

And if you say, you are too old to learn martial arts, then believe me, your firearm is as much a danger to you as it is to others. Let me put this into perspective. More dangerous than a terrorist with a gun, is a civilian with a gun.

To put it simply, it's not enough to build your character, you must also keep your body fit. But mark you, fitness has nothing to do with thinness. A chubby person who works out daily is fitter than a skinny person who has a sedentary lifestyle.

That's why I say, don't just study all the time, go out there and play - baseball first, bible later - build your body as well as your mind. Laziness won't do, for it makes both the body and the mind weak. Discard all laziness and lay down your life for a purpose - a purpose beyond self-obsession.

9. Gun-Fetish (The Sonnet)

Gun-Fetish
(The Sonnet)

When I was in my teenage years,
I believed, having a gun would be so cool.
Then I grew up and it occurred to me,
Firearm fetish is but hysteria of the fool.
Guns don't make the society safe,
Any more than nukes ensure world peace.
Civilians carrying personal firearm,
Are but rabid dogs without a leash.
If you are worried about self-defense,
Daily practice some form of martial arts.
Your gun is not only a threat to you,
It is also a threat to your loved ones.
So I beg you my responsible civilian sibling,
Give up your gun and uphold peacemaking.

ABHIJIT NASKAR

10. Sonnet of Martial Arts

ABHIJIT NASKAR

Sonnet of Martial Arts

The secret to Martial Arts,
Is not style but training.
Pick any form that appeals to you,
And train regularly without failing.
Practice a hundred moves five times,
It is of no use whatsoever.
But practice one move every day,
And it'll be your lifetime protector.
But before all that ask yourself,
Why do you wanna be a martial artist?
Is it to nourish an able mind and body,
Or to be yet another fitness narcissist?
Trash all your arrogance before training.
A martial artist is to be gentle and caring.

11. Dial Down Your Needs

The only way to move the world is to serve the world. You are not going to move the world by being self-obsessed and self-absorbed. Dial down your needs and your power will be endless. Unless we dial down our greed, one crisis or another will continue to rip the heart of humanity apart from inside out.

My needs are less, hence, my dignity is dangerous – my needs are less, hence, my integrity is dangerous. Lesser the needs, greater the peace. World peace comes from individual peace and individual peace comes from individual integrity. What is integrity - a manifestation of humanity - what is humanity - a manifestation of integrity.

When each individual stands up to inhumanity with integrity, justice will prevail on its own, without the need for law and regulation. Let everyone hear – JUSTICE means Just US Trying Individually to Civilize Earth. And how do we civilize earth - by civilizing ourselves, that is, by becoming civilized ourselves.

Summon all potential of civilization that lies unused and dormant within you up to the surface of your awareness and practice them with your last ounce of strength - only then we shall build a civilized world. Remember, it is the entity of action who makes their own destiny, while the coward sits in their couch wailing and praying. Build your destiny my soldier, build it from ground up, and all light will come.

12. The Golden Sonnet

The Golden Sonnet*

Where is el dorado?
It is not a city but a person.
Where is the kingdom of heaven?
It is not a place but compassion.
Where can we find joy?
Not the market but in acts of goodness.
Where can we find health?
Not in gadgets but in simpleness.
Where can we find strength?
Not in the bank but in character.
How can we make progress?
Not with luxury but by lifting the other.
Lesser the needs, better the life.
Gentler the soul, lighter the strife.

*I wrote this sonnet originally in Spanish, entitled
"El Soneto Dorado", then rewrote in English.

13. El Soneto Dorado

El Soneto Dorado

¿Donde esta el dorado?
No es una ciudad, es una persona.
¿Donde esta el cielo?
No es un lugar, es conducta.
¿Dónde está la felicidad?
No está en el mercado, está en bondad.
¿Dónde está la salud?
No está en máquinas, está en simpleza.
¿Qué es la fuerza?
No está la billetera, está personaje.
¿Qué es el progreso?
No es lujo, es el bienestar de la gente.
Menores necesidades, mejor la vida.
Más suave el alma, más ligera la lucha.

14. When You Defy Inclusion

You cannot believe in civilization till you become civilization. There cannot be any civilization unless you are willing to live as the civilization personified. Be brave, get hold of yourself, and march forward - march forward with an expansive spirit, defying everything that facilitates sectarianism.

Let me put this into perspective with the example of our own United States of America. No diversity, no America. No assimilation, no America. No inclusion, no America. And though I used our America as an example, the fact of the matter is, this simple principle of societal growth applies to not just America, but every nation on earth. Any nation that defies inclusion, signs its own death warrant. Defiance of inclusion is defiance of life, for defiance of inclusion is defiance of diversity and diversity is life itself.

Therefore, defiance of inclusion in the name of national security, doesn't actually ensure national security, it only halts a nation's growth. And that is the fundamental flaw in the study of international relations - it tries of instill a kind of nonsectarian relations amongst nations, while acting out of sectarian interests.

To have real, practical, functional international relations, we must act as a people of a planet first, then if we so desire, as people of nations. But again, we can't stand still just there, for this too applies till we come into contact with other intelligent lifeforms. And believe me, we will – someday, if we survive that long as a species that is.

As I said, expansion is the key - no expansion, no ascension. Rigidity, orthodoxy, all these must go. Remember, wishful thinking won't make this world a better place, mindful thinking and heartful action will.

Think with your mind, act with your heart. Past is past for a reason, it belongs behind. You may care for it, you may learn from it, but you must never live in it. Life is in the present and present is alive when it evolves. Hence, a mind is alive only when it learns from the past, aims towards the future, and lives in the present.

15. Flag Cruelty Fraught
(The New American Anthem)

Flag Cruelty Fraught
(The New American Anthem)

Say, can you see,
The darkness we've caused?
Our star spangled banner,
Is a flag cruelty fraught.
It ain't land of the free,
It ain't home of the brave.
Where looks define dignity,
Is but humanity's grave.
Slavery is alive as racism,
Bigotry still claims dominion.
First we must treat these ailments,
Or else, for us there is no dawn.
O say, it's time to abolish all false glory.
Forget valor, let's first practice equality.

16. Sonnet of Climate Change

Sonnet of Climate Change

No matter whether you are loaded,
All the world's money won't save your child.
As our climate gets further compromised,
The rich and poor will suffer and die alike.
Industry gave us affluence and advancement,
But at the expense of our planet's wellbeing.
Our ancestors couldn't fathom it back then,
We don't have their luxury to be greedy fiend.
We barely have a decade to reduce emission,
After that all the prayers won't rescue humanity.
You think things have been hard in your life,
Wait till you hear in grave your children's agony.
Enough with this bickering over phony regulation!
Discard all luxury and reduce individual emission.

17. Present is Life

The present is life - all else is either memory or imagination. And though we are a product of our memory, it doesn't mean we are bound to that memory - for we have the capacity to make new memory - in which lies our capacity for growth. So though it is only logical to accept our memory of the past as part of our identity, we must never be stuck in them.

Whether it is a memory of faith and rituals, whether it is a memory of culture and ethnicity, whether it is a memory of heritage and traditions - life must reign over all memories of the past, for when life reigns over the past, love will reign over the present – love will reign over the world.

Let me put it another way. Be a love-nut, not a faith-freak - be a light-bringer, not a peddler of dark - be a lifter of the world, not a drag on the world.

The fate of the world is predicated on the actions of the few brave beings who can sacrifice all towards a purpose without bothering with material abundance. And it is their sacrifice that enables the rest of humanity to live in a civilized world. I have been mocked and ridiculed my whole life, but know this, those who mock me today, their children will thank me tomorrow.

It is only through extraordinary obstacles and heart-crunching ridicule that we can achieve extraordinary greatness. That is why, it is no cup of tea of the cowards, it requires brave souls, who can walk on fiery charcoal every day of their life and yet lend a hand to those in need with a smile on their face.

You see, those who really work for society, care for neither applause nor mockery, all they care for is to see the fallen stand up and walk again. But make not the mistake of thinking that they don't feel the joy of applause and agony of ridicule - they surely do, for they are human after all, but what sets them apart from the masses is that they continue to work through both applause and ridicule without indulging in either of them.

18. What Are We

ABHIJIT NASKAR

Now the question is, how come non-indulgence comes to action only in a handful of individuals, and not the whole of the human population? And the answer is quite simple - so long as personal benefit is your foremost priority, you are bound to be swayed by applause and devastated by ridicule, but once you expand the self to engulf the whole society, the benefit of society automatically becomes more important to you than your own benefit, and when the benefit of society is your foremost priority, you are no longer swayed by applause or devastated by ridicule, for now something else is way more important to you than all the praise and mockery in the world - it is the uplift of your society.

Let me put it another way. So long as you are self-obsessed, applause and mockery will equally impair your capacity. Wipe out every trace of self-obsession and you'll learn to work through both applause and mockery - and you'll rise as the true victor of time.

So, I say to you – be one with every place and every person, and from that oneness will rise justice, equality and harmony. The more oneness you are able to manifest in your heart, the greater impact you'll have over society.

But mark you, oneness is not exactly an ability, it is accountability in action, just like, accountability is oneness in action. Each is a reflection of the other. If you just feel one, the other will appear on its own, for in practice, they are one and the same. Oneness is accountability, accountability is oneness.

What are we? Expression of oneness. What if we don't feel one? We are not alive. Everything civilized that you can think of, is a manifestation of oneness. Inclusion - a manifestation of oneness. Harmony - a manifestation of oneness. Equality - a manifestation of oneness. Justice - a manifestation of oneness. Progress - a manifestation of oneness.

And the road to oneness goes through people, for people are the very road. So, don't be lost in pleasure, for they don't last long, be lost in people, and you'll find eternal joy. All assume that the purpose of life is happiness - it's not - happiness is only a byproduct of service. The world needs service, the world needs sacrifice. Sacrifice is the law of uplift. I have said this before, I'll say it again. Without sacrifice, there can be no civilization - without sacrifice, there can be no progress.

19. Watchwords of Excellence

Security, comfort, luxury, all these are the aim of the coward, whereas, the civilized being of character aims for self-correction, integrity and collective growth. However, the trouble with our world is that, it is built on a paradigm that facilitates and rewards shallowness, and vilifies selflessness.

So what is the way out? The transformation of all paradigms lies in the individual. To put it simply - if you want the paradigm to change, you must live as a walking example of that change. So, to reform this self-obsessed hell into a heaven of unselfishness, you must become unselfish yourself.

What this means is that, you must bring down all sectarian walls inside your heart, and contain the whole world into your chest. When the heart learns to contain the whole world within itself, or we should say, when the heart unlearns every bit of selfishness that keeps it from assimilating the world, that's when the animal goes to sleep and the human wakes up.

Struggle, struggle, struggle - sacrifice, sacrifice, sacrifice - these are the watchwords of excellence. And it is with excellence that we'll revolutionize our world, not with success. Look at all those successful people - not a single concern for the downtrodden - not a single act of genuine compassion for those who have nothing - if this is success, then let me remain unsuccessful the rest of my life while struggling to elevate my society.

If there is an iota of humanity in you, throw all ambition of success overboard and give yourself fully to the rejuvenation of your society. A life of struggle spent in service is far greater than a life of comfort spent in self-obsession.

Struggle my friend - struggle till the last breath in your body - for only when a handful of lionhearts struggle through their whole life for the betterment of others, can the children of tomorrow live in a civilized dawn.

It is very easy to be a proud descendant, what takes character is to be a responsible ancestor. Be a responsible ancestor my friend. Plant a sapling so that someday it provides shelter to others. You may not get to sit in its shade, so what! You are human not when you work solely to lift yourself, you are human when you work with the genuine desire to lift others.

20. Modern Meditation

You may feel weak at times. And that's good, because being weak at times is a sign of being human. Don't resist weakness, embrace it, and work through it. Work is the only antidote to weakness. And remember, the only weakness is to think of yourself as weak - strength is to work through weakness.

However, if your work, i.e. your job is only a means for you to earn a living, nothing more, then the most effective way out of weakness is through meditation.

But mark you, by meditation I don't mean sit straight and mutter aum and stuff like some mindless parrot, rather I mean, engage in something where you can be lost - music for example. However, if crouching down like a corpse and chanting mantras is what appeals to you, then that's completely fine. But do not make the barbarian mistake to assume that that's what meditation is all about. Meditation has nothing to do with crouching and chanting, meditation means losing oneself in activity - any activity of one's own choosing – mental or physical.

Music is meditation, painting is meditation, dancing is meditation, math is meditation - any act that helps you lose yourself and elevates your mind in the process, is an act of meditation. So throw away all rigid and traditional definitions and dogmas of meditation and just do something to be lost, for when you lose yourself, you'll find yourself.

Our attachment to tradition must be abolished from its very root, only then shall we be able to distinguish the bad from the good within those traditions. Remember o brave soldier, each of us must be the maker of modern earth, and for that, three things are needed - reason, courage and warmth.

Rigidity, prejudice, assumption - all these must go. Allegiance of any kind must be thrown away. Let me give you an example. Time for King James and Uncle Sam has long gone, now it's time for King Conscience and Mother Earth. If you don't realize this simple fact, then I have nothing to say to you - so you better throw my work in the trash and keep clinging to your beloved scripture and nationality till the whole world burns to ashes in your petty nationalistic, religious and cultural squabbles.

Attach yourself to society, the whole, radiant society, with all its diversity, not to some puny, little tribe. Keep your scripture if you must, keep your constitution if you must, but never let them be a hindrance to your humanity. Tribal rigidity and civilized humanity are antithesis of each other.

21. Selflessness Over Recklessness

The idea of selflessness is becoming rare, while recklessness and self-obsession are grabbing hold of the social psyche. This can't be. We mustn't let it be, for if it continues, then despite all the magnificent marvels of science and technology, humankind will be the loneliest and most divided species of all.

So I call upon all the humans everywhere - humans mark you, not human looking savages - stand up and say out loud - enough! The world begins with the individual. Once you realize this, the road to reform will appear to you on its own. Reform is born of the reformer, not the other way around.

But here's the thing, the road will appear alright as you start living the life of a reformer, however, it will by no means be covered with petals of praise, instead every step of the way you'll face nothing but disappointment and ridicule. Endure my friend - lose not your zeal my friend, for today's mockery is tomorrow's applause.

Besides, we don't die for society for the applause, we die so the humans yet to be born may have a world less savage than ours. With

ABHIJIT NASKAR

your last drop of sweat and blood work to better the lives of others no matter the agony, for if there is no reformer, there will be no civilization.

And those who think it's the mindless masses driven by greed and security who make this world worth living in, they have another thing coming. Reformers who have done away with all greed and security are the real keepers and makers of society. So, be a reformer my friend - be a reformer with a heart of honey and nerves of thunder.

Always remember, transformation first, tradition later - reason first, rituals later - character first, cash later - people first, pedestal later. If you can work even five minutes lifting others, you'll live a lifetime in those five minutes.

22. Be Unrealistic (The Sonnet)

Be Unrealistic
(The Sonnet)

Be unrealistic and work for a world,
That the society considers nonsense.
Once upon a time taming fire was unreal,
Then arose a bunch of brave sentience.
Today's madness is tomorrow's sanity,
If we're mad enough to stand solo on guard.
Today's sacrifice is tomorrow's civilization,
If we can give all without hoping reward.
If only one person dies for the cause,
A hundred people realize their humanity.
I may die today in the line of duty,
But the struggle continues through eternity.
So let us be brave and go beyond reality.
Let us be accountable and do the necessary.

23. Love Alone Triumphs
(The Sonnet)

Love Alone Triumphs
(The Sonnet)

Great people have often said,
Truth alone triumphs.
I am no great but a plain human,
So I say, love alone triumphs.
Truth may require intellect,
Inquiry requires some cynicism.
To be loving needs none of that,
Love lights up the darkest chasm.
Keep your intellect if you desire,
Explore further the arc of truth.
But all the discovery means nothing,
If countless souls go without food.
It is far better to be an insane lover,
Than to be a heartless discoverer.

24. Lift Others (The Sonnet)

Lift Others
(The Sonnet)

If you want to lift your spirit,
Lift others.
If you want to help yourself,
Help others.
If you want to find happiness,
Forget about happiness.
If you want to discover joy,
Just give without selfishness.
Be crazy, loco and bonkers,
For the welfare of others.
The only kingdom of heaven,
Is in cheering someone who suffers.
Better than self-help is unself-help,
For the rise of people is rise of the self.

25. What is Goodness

Life isn't measured in years, it's measured in acts of goodness. But the question is, what is goodness? Is it a habit? Is it a skill? Is it a philosophy? For example, many people often send me emails saying that they've been reading a lot on living a life of service, yet they can't figure out where to begin! I tell them, you can't figure out where to begin because you think of service like you think of any other notion in life, as a philosophy or a skill - you don't read about a life of service, you live it.

It is an act driven by sheer accountability, which is practically love in action. So when you genuinely feel a sense of love towards the society, like the way you feel towards your partner or children, you won't have to read about goodness and service, they'll pour out of your hands and feet like water from a fountain.

For ages, religion has been trying to bind the idea of love and service in a single book, and in the process they've only destroyed their very essence. Remember this, any book that claims to be a book of life and love while demanding absolute obedience is but a book of death and degradation.

You may read about various matters of life to be acquainted with how others have thought and felt about them, but never let yourself be enslaved by books - never. Love is to be felt and lived, not read and learnt. Bookworms love to say, there is no friend as loyal as a book. I say, if your knowledge of all those books doesn't come to any use of the people around you, then there's no creature as selfish as you. Better an illiterate lover of humanity, than a septic tank of intellectual stupidity.

I'll put it to you in simple words. If you can give your hand to some, it doesn't matter whether you are handsome. It is the heart that defines the beauty of a person, not the body or the brain. But the question is, can you actually practice this simple principle in your everyday life?

For example, can you act the same way with a janitor as you do with a movie star? Can you speak to a waitress as sweetly as you speak to a celebrity? Can you be as nice a person to a construction worker as you are to a billionaire? There's no need to judge yourself, but the next time you are in such a situation, simply observe your behavior. And you'll know whether you are really a human or just an animal in human skin.

26. The World is Our Reflection

Seeing yourself in others is the beginning of human life. Once you see yourself in others, right action would appear to you on its own. Then all things civilized will become clear to you as daylight.

See yourself in others and you'll know morality. See yourself in others and you'll know justice. See yourself in others and you'll know serenity. See yourself in others and you'll know progress.

Until then, your mind will continue to play tricks on you with fake morality and righteousness. Let me elaborate with the example of space tourism. Many people are mad at the escapades of billionaires in space, but the fact of the matter is, had they been invited to go with the billionaires themselves, most of them would be thrilled to their bones, for they are not really mad at the billionaires, they are mad because they can't afford such fancy travel.

You see, they are the same people who save up their hard-earned money so they could have a relaxing or thrilling vacation somewhere, even though their version of vacation turns bleak in front of the glorious space vacations of the super-rich.

So to those who pompously ask the question, "should people travel to space for fun", I ask, "should you have a vacation on an island for fun - should you have dinner at a fancy restaurant for fun – when countless souls are suffering from the lack of the very essentials of life?"

It's all about status. A billionaire's idea of vacation is in space, whereas a regular person's idea of a vacation is on some island or in another continent. And if the billionaires are abusing resources for personal enjoyment, so are these regular people.

You have no right to demand moral accountability from billionaires, if you yourself don't mind engaging in your everyday luxuries – for your luxuries may seem dim compared to those of the super-rich, but still the resources you spend on them could feed and clothe at least ten families in developing parts of the world for a year.

The very existence of billionaires is a sign of economic disparities, but they are not the sole cause of those disparities. Every individual engaging in luxury beyond necessity is as much responsible for the economic disparities in society as the super wealthy. So till you learn to distinguish between necessity and luxury and thereafter abolish all trace of luxury from your own life, you are the problem yourself, as much as the greedy capitalists and politicians.

So I say to you, get hold of your own desires first. Observation and modulation - these are the key. But here's the thing, observation and modulation cannot be read or taught, they come on their own, once you become one with your fellow being - once become one with the whole humankind. In short, once you truly see yourself in others, you'll feel disgusted at the very thought of indulging in luxury while countless souls continue to suffer in various parts of the world.

Responsibility comes where there is oneness, and luxury cannot fester where there is responsibility. And that my friend is the solution to all disparities of society - plain, ordinary, everyday responsibility in the individual.

27. Practice The
Religion of Sacrifice

Indifference and disparity go hand in hand. Destroy indifference, and disparity will disappear on its own. All things uncivilized are born of indifference-induced separation - separation between you and society. When you and society are one, all is well and civilized with the world, but when you and society are separate, the world is but a fancy jungle. Separation is bondage, oneness is freedom.

So I say to you again o brave one, never you think that you are different from the society - always remind yourself - I am the society, the society is me. And whatever trace of separation remains is a sign of our primeval selfishness, which can only be overpowered by our desire for sacrifice. Each of us must turn into a living flame of sacrifice, only then will the children of tomorrow live in the first light of civilization.

Remember this, sacrifice makes a human out of an animal. Those who are empty, talk about etiquettes, those with character, don't talk unnecessarily, they sacrifice for those in need. With selfishness we sow the seeds of our own ruin, wipe out all selfishness, and growth will come, joy will come, life will come.

The only religion that is to be practiced is the religion of sacrifice for the helpless, the oppressed, the forgotten. What is civilization? It is the product of sacrifice. Today's sacrifice is tomorrow's civilization. Today's service is tomorrow's serenity. Dare to serve, dare to sacrifice, and you'll be thanked by countless generations to come.

Those who think ahead of their time are always ridiculed by their own time. Mind not the ridicule, mind not the mockery. Remember, those who can't do, mock, those who do, have no time to mock. That is why, I do not respond to mockery and ridicule. I only smile and move on.

Know this, if you are sincere in your desire for the good of others, then nothing can stand in your way. A hundred mountains will crumble to dust in front of your resolve. Such is the strength of a determined mind. Such is the glory of a pure and uncorrupted beacon of sacrifice.

28. Only The Servants Rule

Not all minds are human. A human mind is one that lives among the humans - a human mind is one that lives for the humans. So, fly away home my friend - from the grovel pit of segregation, into the heart of the humans. Nothing else matters – not culture, not nationality, not faith - nothing. They are all irrelevant.

When I talk about humans, I mean humans - all humans - without exception. The so-called puny identities concocted by a narrowminded society mean absolutely nothing as far as civilization and progress are concerned. Let me give you a simple, everyday example. I use shampoo for haircare, but the shampoo is not my identity, likewise I use a passport for travel, but the passport is not my identity.

The name's Naskar, and if you think your pathetic little labels of faith, nation and culture can define even a syllable of it, you've got another thing coming. The name is Naskar and Naskar is a human - so are you - so is every single being with conscience and character.

However, those who choose to live as tribal savages in fancy clothes, I won't argue with them, nor do I have any grudge against them - for change is born of example, not of argumentation. I've got no time for argumentation. The only way to turn this savage tribal world into a civilized human world is to be civilized humans ourselves.

Remember, only the servants rule the world - only the servants live. Or to put it simply, service is life - service is salvation. We are all candles, our purpose is to burn for others. But mark you, by others, I don't mean the rich, pompous and famous, for the vast majority of the population are already there to lick their boots anyway, rather I mean those suffering at the bottom of the social ladder, who don't even have the ability to pull themselves up by their bootstraps, for they don't even have boots. Serve them my friend - burn for them - be annihilated for them. That's your mission as a being of conscience - that's your mission as a being of character - that's your mission as a human.

You may be a teacher, you may be a janitor, you may be a waitress, you may be a scientist, preacher or artist –whatever you are, whatever you do, do it for the people – so that those who have nothing, can learn to walk again, smile again, live again, because of you.

29. People over Popularity

Let me tell you a story. Once in an airplane I met a movie actor. I usually do not sleep on flights, even if they are long-haul, either I watch a movie or get some writing done. This particular time, I was working on my laptop taking down some notes for a book. The actor was on the seat next to me. After observing my writing for a while he approached me himself, and asked whether I am a writer. I wasn't quite popular yet back then. I replied, I am a scientist and I do write as well. He then said, "I'm surely gonna read some of your work, it seems fascinating." Then he extended his hand to shake mine and introduced himself. I shook his hand and said "I like your work too." Then there was an awkward silence - perhaps he expected that I'd ask him for a selfie. When I didn't even after a few seconds, he looked a little surprised. However, we spent the rest of the flight chatting.

You see, only the shallow go bonkers over someone's fame and celebrity. I'd rather share emotions with a person and make memories than take selfies with no emotions and memories. Take selfies if you like, but never confuse selfies with sentiments. Remember, the purpose of a photograph is to remind you of a memory, but if there is no memory to be reminded of, then what's the point of all those photographs!

Communicate with people, hear from them, learn about them, then after that if you like, take a selfie as a memento. Live in the moment, not in the cloud.

Focus on people, not on their status. Focus on character, not on clothes. Foster kinship over skinship. It is a common tendency of the animal within us to be attracted to body and status, in the subconscious pursuit of self-preservation. If you are to call yourself human, you must first rise above such tendency.

How you ask? To question such tendency against the anticipation of pleasure is to defeat them. Once you learn to question the animal within, in time you'd automatically start to see the sheer savagery of those tendencies, and that very act of self-observation and self-regulation is the awakening of the human.

You eat so you could sustain the body, but what good is that body if it doesn't come to the aid of others. You read so you sustain the mind, but what good is that mind if it doesn't come to the aid of others! Struggle my friend, struggle - not for the betterment of yourself, but for the betterment of those around you - for the betterment of your society. That is practical religion, that is practical divinity, that is practical humanism.

30. No Rest (The Sonnet)

No Rest

(The Sonnet)

There is no rest,
Till the last drop of tear is wiped out.
There is no leisure,
Till the voiceless can speak aloud.
There is no relaxing,
Till the last empty stomach is fed.
There is no sleep,
Till all droopy spines are made straight.
There is no joy,
Till the last grey life is colored.
There is no comfort,
Till the last anxious soul is empowered.
The struggle isn't over till the fallen rise.
Security later, first let us be civilized.

31. Pain over Pleasure

Person practicing humanity defies all sectarian identity and says without fear – hola, soy GORA - Guerrero, Observador, Reformador, Amante - or - I am the World - Warrior, Observer, Reformer, Lover, Diviner. Be that human my friend and give yourself as a living sacrifice to the real mission impossible on earth - the mission of alleviating suffering and inhumanity.

But by suffering I don't mean the shallow suffering of those living in the lap of comfort and luxury. I am talking about the real suffering of planet earth - suffering caused by the lack of essentials. Here some egotistical snob living in luxury may argue, who am I to say that the suffering of the wealthy is not real! To which I say, like any living person on earth, the privileged as well have their own real suffering, but the fact of the matter is, most of their suffering is born of self-obsession. Most of their suffering constitutes things like not having wifi for half an hour or running out of battery on the phone or not being able to upgrade to the latest smartphone till the next paycheck.

There's an entire group of professionals who have made a living out of the insecurities and snobberies of the privileged. They sell motivation to these pompous snobs, so that the entitled and self-absorbed portion of society could remain entitled and self-absorbed for the rest of their life.

I'll say it to you plainly, I am not here to motivate you, I am here to remind you of your human duty. Or let me put it another way. I don't write to inspire you, I write to destroy you, because without the bravehearts to destroy themselves, there'll be no society.

And whatever real suffering the privileged have, would go down exponentially on their own once they stop indulging in self-obsession and use their privilege to lift others.

What we are talking about here is the suffering of those forgotten by the capitalistic circles of society. To alleviate their suffering is to be our highest purpose in life, for this is the sign of real, practical progress. Let us be the most progressive people that ever walked the planet, with our firm sense of reason accompanied by a revolutionary gentleness. In doing so we'll have to bear unbearable pain - so what! Unbearable pain delivers unthinkable ascension.

Pick up a pebble and hit your forehead with it gently. Does it hurt? Why? Because you are alive. But does the pebble feel the same pain as you? Why not? Because it has no life. To put it simply, life and pain go together - if you feel no pain, you are not alive. People ask me, how to deal with pain and negative thoughts? I smile and reply, what are you, mind or machine? Don't try to avoid pain, and don't crave for too much pleasure. Work your purpose through both pain and pleasure without paying either of them much attention.

So long as you live, you'll have to bear pain - make sure it is for a grand purpose. Average people measure themselves by the amount of pleasure they can buy for themselves, reformers measure themselves by the amount of pain they can bear for others. The greatest of all pleasures is to bear pain for others.

32. Hola, Soy GORA
(The Sonnet)

Hola, Soy GORA
(The Sonnet)

Hermanas y hermanos, hola, soy GORA,
Guerrero, Observador, Reformador, Amante.
Thus speaks the human practicing humanity,
Despite all agony, no retrocedas oh valiente!
To the helpless, destitute and discriminated,
I am but a nameless servant most humble.
To lift the fallen and make them self-reliant,
Is the purpose of my life, straight and simple.
Beware o peddlers of hate and bigotry,
Get hold of your prejudice and hysteria!
When calm, reformist mind brings light,
When enraged, it is the fabled chupacabra!
Each conscientious being is reform incarnate.
From your humane struggle never you deviate.

33. Mind Before Mars

Give your last drop of water to someone thirsty, give your last crumb of bread to someone hungry, and you'll be human - for the first time in your life, you'll pass from non-existence to existence. There is no existence except in service. There is no rest except in sacrificial restlessness. There is no serenity except in willful annihilation of one's own serenity for the smile of others.

People have a tendency to either fundamentalize things or philosophize things - those who fundamentalize things, boast about heritage, and those who philosophize things, boast about intellect. I say, neither heritage nor intellect is to be placed at the supreme altar of the human mind, instead what we must place in our mind's altar is people.

This is the task of our life - to place people at our mind's altar and serve them with all our heart as our deity. Life of comfort is a life in vain, life of luxury is a life most lame, life of service is a life most sane. Remember, there is no use in travelling to the moon and mars, if the distance between mind and mind remains ever-growing. I am not against space-exploration, but if we are to speak of priorities - mind before mars, that's the motto. If your child or your spouse is sick, you won't be spending your money on a sports car will you?

Mere external travel won't make us an advanced lifeform, we must first erase the distance amongst each other. A sectarian species, whether they live on earth or mars, is still a sectarian species. All the stars will lay at our feet if we just rid ourselves of our selfishness. And that is the first and foremost duty of a human being - to rid oneself of selfishness. Biologically it may be impossible to do so completely, but the very acknowledgment and conscious effort thereof, incapacitate a great deal of that selfishness.

Selfishness will always be there, for no magic can make it disappear from our millions of years old neuroanatomy, but you choose whether you are going to act on that selfishness like mindless machines or stand up as a true being of humanity. I'll say it to you plainly. If selfishness enters, humanity is gone. If you ask me, can I define humanity? I'll tell you, I can - in one word - selflessness.

BIBLIOGRAPHY

Archer M., (2000), Being Human: The Problem of Agency. Cambridge University Press.

Archer M., (2003), Structure, Agency and the Internal Conversation. Cambridge University Press.

Adolphs R (2003) Cognitive neuroscience of human social behaviour. Nature Rev Neurosci 4: 165–178.

Adolphs R, Tranel D, Damasio AR (2003) Dissociable neural systems for recognizing emotions. Brain Cogn 52: 61–69.

Afton, A. D. (1985). Forced copulation as a reproductive strategy of male lesser scaup: A field test of some predictions. - Behaviour 92, p. 146-167.

Allison T, Puce A, McCarthy G. (2000) Social perception from visual cues: role of the STS region. Trends Cogn Sci 4: 267–278.

Andresen, Jensine, and Robert Forman, eds. Cognitive Models and Spiritual Maps. Bowling Green, Ohio: Imprint Academic, 2000.

Ashbrook, James, and Carol Albright. The Humanizing Brain: Where Religion and Neuroscience Meet. Cleveland, OH: Pilgrim Press, 1997.

Azari, Nina, Janpeter Nickel, Gilbert Wunderlich, Michael Niedeggen, Harald Hefter, Lutz Tellmann, Hans Herzog, Petra Stoerig, Dieter Birnbacher, and Rudiger Seitz. "Neural Correlates of Religious Experience." European Journal of Neuroscience 13, no. 8 (2001)

Agar, N. (2004). Liberal eugenics: In defence of human enhancement. London: Blackwell Publishing.

Alteheld, N., Roessler, G., Vobig, M., & Walter, R. (2004). The retina implant new approach to a visual prosthesis. Biomedizinische Technik, 49(4), 99–103.

Antal, A., Nitsche, M. A., Kincses, T. Z., Kruse, W., Hoffmann, K. P., & Paulus, W. (2004a). Facilitation of visuo-motor learning by transcranial direct current stimulation of the motor and extrastriate visual areas in humans. European Journal of Neuroscience, 19(10), 2888–2892.

Bernstein R.J., (1971), Praxis and Action: Contemporary Philosophies of Human Activity. Philadelphia: University of Pennsylvania Press.

Bernstein R.J., (1976), The Restructuring Social and Political Thought.

Bernstein R.J., (1983), Beyond Relativism and Objectivism: Science, Hermeneutics, and Praxis. Philadelphia: University of Pennsylvania Press.

Bernstein R.J., (1986), Philosophical Profiles. Philadelphia: University of Pennsylvania Press.

Bernstein R.J., (1991), New Constellation. Cambridge: MIT Press.

Birkhead, T. R., Johnson, S. D. & Nettleship, D. N. (1985). Extra-pair matings and mate guarding in the common murre Uria aalge. - Anim. Behav. 33, p. 608-619.

Beauregard, Mario, and Vincent Paquette. "Neural Correlates of a Mystical Experience in Carmelite Nuns." Neuroscience Letters 405, no. 3 (2006)

Benson, Herbert. Timeless Healing: The Power and Biology of Belief. New York: Scribner, 1996

Bose, Subhas Chandra. An Indian Pilgrim: An Unfinished Autobiography, Oxford University Press, 1997

Bose, Subhas Chandra. The Indian Struggle 1920-1942, Oxford University Press, 1997

Bogen, J.E.(1995a), 'On the neurophysiology of consciousness: Part I. An overview', Consciousness and Cognition, 4.

Bogen, J.E. (1995b), 'On the neurophysiology of consciousness: Part II. Constraining the semantic problem', Consciousness and Cognition, 4.

Bremner, J. D., R. Soufer, et al. (2001). "Gender differences in cognitive and neural correlates of remembrance of emotional words." Psychopharmacol Bull 35 (3).

Brothers, L. (2002). The social brain: A project for integrating primate behavior and neurophysiology in a new domain. In J. T. Cacioppo et al. (Eds.), Foundations in neuroscience. Cambridge, MA: MIT Press.

Buss, D. D. (2003). Evolutionary Psychology: The New Science of Mind, 2nd ed. New York: Allyn & Bacon.

Buss, D. M. (1989). "Conflict between the sexes: Strategic interference and the evocation of anger and upset." J Pers Soc Psychol 56 (5).

Buss, D. M. (1995). "Psychological sex differences. Origins through sexual selection." Am Psychol 50 (3).

Buss, D. M. (2002). "Review: Human Mate Guarding." Neuro Endocrinol Lett 23 (Suppl 4).

Buss, D. M., and D. P. Schmitt (1993). "Sexual strategies theory: An evolutionary perspective on human mating." Psychol Rev 100 (2).

Blakemore SJ, Decety J (2001) From the perception of action to the understanding of intention. Nature Rev Neurosci 2: 561.

Bruce C, Desimone R, Gross CG (1981) Visual properties of neurons in a polysensory area in superior temporal sulcus of the macaque. J Neurophysiol 46: 369–384.

Buccino G, Vogt S, Ritzl A, Fink GR, Zilles K, Freund HJ, Rizzolatti G (2004) Neural circuits underlying imitation of hand actions: an event related fMRI study. Neuron 42: 323–34.

Colapietro V., (1988), "Human Agency: The Habits of Our Being." Southern Journal of Philosophy, XXVI, 2, pp. 153-68.

Colapietro V., (1992), "Purpose, Power, and Agency." The Monist, 75, 4 (October) pp. 423-44.

Colapietro V., (2004a), "C. S. Peirce's Reclamation of Teleology." Nature in American Philosophy, ed. Jean De Groot (Washington, D.C.: Catholic University Press of America), pp. 88-108.

Colapietro V., (2004b), "Portrait of a Historicist: An Alternative Reading of Peircean Semiotic." Semiotiche, 2/04 [maggio 2004], pp. 49-68.

Colapietro V., (2006), "Engaged Pluralism: Between Alterity and Sociality." The Pragmatic Century: Conversations with Richard J. Bernstein (Albany, NY: SUNY Press), pp. 39-68.

Carey DP, Perrett DI, Oram MW (1997) Recognizing, understanding and reproducing actions. In: Jeannerod M, Grafman J (eds) Handbook of neuropsychology. Vol. 11: Action and cognition. Elsevier, Amsterdam.

Carr L, Iacoboni M, Dubeau MC, Mazziotta JC, Lenzi GL (2003) Neural mechanisms of empathy in humans: a relay from neural systems for imitation to limbic areas. Proc Natl Acad Sci USA 100: 5497–5502.

Changeux JP, Ricoeur P (1998) La nature et la règle. Odile Jacob, Paris.

Chomsky Noam, (2017) Requiem for the American Dream

Chomsky Noam, (2016) Who Rules the World?

Chomsky Noam, (2010) How the World Works

Churchland, P.S. (1986), Neurophilosophy (Cambridge, MA: The MIT Press).

Churchland, P.S. & Ramachandran, V.S. (1993), 'Filling in: Why Dennett is wrong', in Dennett and His Critics: Demystifying Mind, ed. B. Dahlbom (Oxford: Blackwell Scientific Press).

Churchland, P.S., Ramachandran, V.S. & Sejnowski, T.J. (1994), 'A critique of pure vision', in Large- scale Neuronal Theories of the Brain, ed. C. Koch & J.L. Davis (Cambridge, MA: The MIT Press).

Coyle EF. Integration of the physiological factors determining endurance performance ability. Exerc Sport Sci Rev. 1995;23:25–63.

Crick, F. (1994), The Astonishing Hypothesis: The Scientific Search for the Soul (New York: Simon and Schuster).

Crick, F. (1996), 'Visual perception: rivalry and consciousness', Nature, 379.

Crick, F. & Koch, C. (1992), 'The problem of consciousness', Scientific American, 267.

Craig AD (2002) How do you feel? Interoception: the sense of the physiological condition of the body. Nature Rev Neurosci 3: 655–666.

Damasio, A (2003a) Looking for Spinoza. Harcourt Inc. Damasio A (2003b) Feeling of emotion and the self. Ann NY Acad Sci 1001: 253–261.

d'Aquili, Eugene. "Senses of Reality in Science and Religion." Zygon 17, no 4 (1982)

d'Aquili, Eugene. "The Biopsychological Determinants of Religious Ritual Behavior." Zygon 10, no. 1 (1975)

d'Aquili, Eugene. "The Myth-Ritual Complex: A Biogenetic Structural Analysis." Zygon 18, no. 3 (1983)

d'Aquili, Eugene, and Andrew Newberg. The Mystical Mind: Probing the Biology of Religious Experience. Minneapolis: Fortress Press, 1999.

Daly DD. 1958. Ictal affect. Am J Psychiatry.

Damasio, A. (1994) Descartes' Error: Emotion, Reason and the Human Brain. New York, Putnams.

Damasio, A. (1999) The Feeling of What Happens: Body, Emotion and the Making of Consciousness. London, Heinemann.

Darwin, C. (1859) On the Origin of Species by Means of Natural Selection. London, Murray.

Darwin, C. (1871) The Descent of Man and Selection in Relation to Sex. London, John Murray.

Darwin, C. (1872) The Expression of the Emotions in Man and Animals. London, John Murray; also published 1965, Chicago, University of Chicago Press.

Dawkins, M.S. (1987) Minding and mattering. In C. Blakemore and S. Greenfield (eds) Mindwaves. Oxford, Blackwell, 151-60.

Dawkins, R. (1976) The Selfish Gene. Oxford, Oxford University Press; a new edition, with additional material, was published in 1989.

Dawkins, R. (1986) The Blind Watchmaker. London, Longman.

Di Pellegrino G, Fadiga L, Fogassi L, Gallese V, Rizzolatti G (1992) Understanding motor events: A neurophysiological study. Exp Brain Res 91: 176–80.

Deikman, A.J. (2000) A functional approach to mysticism. Journal of Consciousness Studies 7(11-12), 75-91.

Delmonte, M.M. (1987) Personality and meditation. In M. West (ed.) The Psychology of Meditation. Oxford, Clarendon Press, 118-32.

Dennett, D.C. (1988) Quining qualia. In A.J. Marcel and E. Bisiach (eds) Consciousness in Contemporary Science. Oxford, Oxford University Press, 42-77.

Dennett, D.C. (1991) Consciousness Explained. Boston, MA, and London, Little, Brown and Co.

Dennett, D.C. (1995a) Darwin's Dangerous Idea. London, Penguin.

Dennett, D.C. (1995b) The unimagined preposterousness of zombies. Journal of Consciousness Studies 2(4), 322-6.

Dennett, D.C. (1995c) Cog: steps towards consciousness in robots. In T. Metzinger (ed.) Conscious Experience. Thorverton, Devon, Imprint Academic, 471-87.

Dennett, D.C. (1996a) Facing backwards on the problem of consciousness. Journal of Consciousness Studies 3(1), 4-6.

Dennett, D.C. (1996b) Kinds of Minds: Towards an Understanding of Consciousness. London, Weidenfeld & Nicolson.

Dennett, D.C. (1997) An exchange with Daniel Dennett. In J. Searle (ed.) The Mystery of Consciousness. New York, New York Review of Books, 115-19.

Dennett, D.C. (1998) The myth of double transduction. In S.R. Hameroff, A.W. Kaszniak and A. C. Scott (eds) Toward a Science of Consciousness: The Second Tucson Discussions and Debates. Cambridge, MA, MIT Press, 97-107.

Dennett, D.C. (1998b) Brainchildren: Essays on Designing Minds. Cambridge, MA, MIT Press.

Dennett, D.C. (2001) The fantasy of first person science. Debate with D. Chalmers, Northwestern University, Evanston, IL, February 2001.

Dennett, D.C. (2003) Freedom Evolves. New York, Penguin.

Dennett, D.C. and Kinsbourne, M. (1992) Time and the observer: the where and when of consciousness in the brain. Behavioral and Brain Sciences 15, 183-247, including commentaries and authors' responses.

Dewey J., (1911 [1977]), "Epistemological Realism: The Alleged Ubiquity of the Knowledge Relation." Journal of Philosophy, VIII, 20 (September 28, 1911).

Dewhurst, Kenneth, and A. W. Beard. "Sudden Religious Conversions in Temporal Lobe Epilepsy." British Journal of Psychiatry 117 (1970)

Dewhurst K, Beard AW. Sudden religious conversions in temporal lobe epilepsy. 1970 Epilepsy Behav 2003

Devinsky O, Lai G. Spirituality and religion in epilepsy. Epilepsy Behav 2008.

Devinsky, O., Morrell, MJ, Vogt, BA. (1995) 'Contribution of anterior cingulate cortex to behavior', Brain, 118.

Douglas Stone A., Chapter 24, The Indian Comet, in the book Einstein and the Quantum, Princeton University Press, Princeton, New Jersey, 2013.

E. Horvitz, "One Hundred Year Study on Artificial Intelligence: Reflections and Framing," ed: Stanford University, 2014.

Einstein A. (1925). "Quantentheorie des einatomigen idealen Gases". Sitzungsberichte der Preussischen Akademie der Wissenschaften.

Eckhart Meister, Selected Writings

Egidi R., ed. (1999), "Von Wright and 'Dante's Dream': Stages in a Philosophical Pilgrim's Progress", in In Search of a New Humanism: the Philosophy of G.H. von Wright, ed. by R. Egidi, Kluwer, Dordrecht.

Fadiga L, Fogassi L, Pavesi G, Rizzolatti G (1995) Motor facilitation during action observation: a magnetic stimulation study. J Neurophysiol 73: 2608–2611.

Fogassi L, Gallese V, Fadiga L, Rizzolatti G (1998) Neurons responding to the sight of goal directed hand/arm actions in the parietal area PF (7b) of the macaque monkey. Soc Neurosci Abs 24:257.5.

Frith U, Frith CD (2003) Development and neurophysiology of mentalizing. Philos Trans R Soc Lond B Biol Sci 358: 459.

Farah, M.J. (1989), 'The neural basis of mental imagery', Trends in Neurosciences, 10.

Finlay BL, Darlington RB (1995) Linked regularities in the development and evolution of mammalian brains. Science 268.

Freud, S. "The Interpretation of Dreams", 1900

Freud, S. "Selected papers on hysteria and other psychoneuroses" Journal of Nervous and Mental Disease 1909.

Freud, S. "The Origin and Development of Psychoanalysis", 1910

Freud, S. "Psychopathology of everyday life", 1914

Freud, S. "Beyond the Pleasure Principle", 1920

Frith, C.D. & Dolan, R.J. (1997), 'Abnormal beliefs: Delusions and memory', Paper presented at the May, 1997, Harvard Conference on Memory and Belief.

Gay, Volney, ed. Neuroscience and Religion. Plymouth, UK: Lexington Books, 2009.

Gazzaniga, M. S. (1985). The social brain. New York: Basic Books.

Gazzaniga, M.S. (1993), 'Brain mechanisms and conscious experience', Ciba Foundation Symposium, 174.

Geschwind N. "Behavioural changes in temporal lobe epilepsy". Psychol Med. 1979.

Gellhorn, E., Kiely, W.F. "Mystical states of consciousness: neurophysiological and clinical aspects." J Nerv Ment Dis. 1972;154:399-405.

Gilbert SL, Dobyns WB, Lahn BT (2005) Genetic links between brain development and brain evolution. Nat Rev Genet 6.

Gray JA. The Psychology of Fear and Stress. 2nd ed. New York, NY: Cambridge University Press; 1988.

Gloor, P. (1992), 'Amygdala and temporal lobe epilepsy', in The Amygdala: Neurobiological Aspects of Emotion, Memory and Mental Dysfunction, ed J.P. Aggleton (New York: Wiley-Liss).

Greenspan, S. I. and S. G. Shanker (2004). The first idea: How symbols, language, and intelligence evolved from our early primate ancestors to modern humans. Cambridge, MA: Da Capo Press.

Grady, D. (1993), 'The vision thing: Mainly in the brain', Discover, June.

Gallagher HL, Frith CD (2003) Functional imaging of 'theory of mind'. Trends Cogn Sci 7: 77.

Gallese V, Fogassi L, Fadiga L, Rizzolatti G (2002) Action representation and the inferior parietal lobule. In: Prinz W, Hommel B (eds) Attention & Performance XIX. Common mechanisms in perception and action. Oxford University Press, Oxford.

Gallese V, Keysers C, Rizzolatti G (2004) A unifying view of the basis of social cognition. Trends Cogn Sci 8: 396–403.

Gangitano M, Mottaghy FM, Pascual-Leone A (2001) Phase specific modulation of cortical motor output during movement observation. NeuroReport 12: 1489–1492.

Gangitano M, Mottaghy FM, Pascual-Leone A (2004) Modulation of premotor mirror neuron activity during observation of unpredictable grasping movements. Eur J Neurosci 20: 2193– 2202.

Goldman AI, Sripada CS (2004) Simulationist models of face-based emotion recognition. Cognition 94: 193–213.

Grèzes J, Costes N, Decety J (1998) Top-down effect of strategy on the perception of human biological motion: a PET investigation. Cogn Neuropsychol 15: 553–582.

Grèzes J, Armony JL, Rowe J, Passingham RE (2003) Activations related to "mirror" and "canonical" neurones in the human brain: an fMRI study. Neuroimage 18: 928–937.

Gross CG, Rocha-Miranda CE, Bender DB (1972) Visual properties of neurons in the inferotemporal cortex of the macaque. J Neurophysiol 35: 96–111.

Hari R, Forss N, Avikainen S, Kirveskari S, Salenius S, Rizzolatti G (1998) Activation of human primary motor cortex during action observation: a neuromagnetic study. Proc. Natl Acad Sci USA 95: 15061–15065.

Hardy, G. H. (1940). Ramanujan. Cambridge: Cambridge University Press.

Hall, Daniel, Keith Meador, and Harold Koenig. "Measuring Religiousness in Health Research: Review and Critique." Journal of Religion and Health 47, no. 2 (2008)

Harris, Sam, Jonas Kaplan, Ashley Curiel, Susan Bookheimer, Marco Iacoboni, and Mark Cohen. "The Neural Correlates of Religious and

Nonreligious Belief." PLoS One 4, no. 10 (October 1, 2009)

Halgren, E. (1992), 'Emotional neurophysiology of the amygdala within the context of human cognition', in The Amygdala: Neurobiological Aspects of Emotion, Memory and Mental Dysfunction, ed J.P. Aggleton (New York: Wiley-Liss).

Halligan PW, Fink GR, Marshal JC, Vallar G. 2003. Spatial cognition: evidence from visual neglect. Trends Cogn Sci.

Handbook of Emotions, Edited by Michael Lewis, Jeannette M. Haviland-Jones, and Lisa Feldman Barrett, The Guilford Press; 3rd edition (2010).

Hameroff, S.R. and Penrose, R. (1996) Conscious events as orchestrated space-time selections. Journal of Consciousness Studies 3(1), 36-53; also reprinted in J. Shear (ed.) (1997) Explaining Consciousness-The Hard

Problem. Cambridge, MA, MIT Press, 177-95.

Harding, D.E. (1961) On Having no Head: Zen and the Re-Discovery of the Obvious. London, Buddhist Society.

Hardy, A. (1979) The Spiritual Nature of Man: A Study of Contemporary Religious Experience. Oxford, Clarendon Press.

Harre, R. and Gillett, G. (1994) The Discursive Mind. Thousand Oaks, CA, Sage.

Haugeland, J. (ed.) (1997) Mind Design II: Philosophy, Psychology, Artificial Intelligence. Cambridge, MA, MIT Press.

Hauser, M.D. (2000) Wild Minds: What Animals Really Think. New York, Henry Holt and Co.; London, Penguin.

Hebb, D.O. (1949) The Organization of Behavior. New York, Wiley.

Helmholtz, H.L.F. von (1856-67) Treatise on Physiological Optics.

Hess, EH (1975) "The role of pupil size in communication," Scientific American, 233(5), 110–12.

Heyes, C.M. (1998) Theory of mind in nonhuman primates. Behavioral and Brain Sciences 21, 101-48; with commentaries.

Heyes, C.M. and Galef, B.G. (eds) (1996) Social Learning in Animals: The Roots of Culture. San Diego, CA, Academic Press.

Hilgard, E.R. (1986) Divided Consciousness: Multiple Controls in Human Thought and Action. New York, Wiley.

Hilton, E.N., Lundberg, T.R. Transgender Women in the Female Category of Sport: Perspectives on Testosterone Suppression and Performance Advantage. Sports Med 51, 199–214 (2021).

Hitler, Adolf. Mein Kampf, 1925

Hodgson, R. (1891) A case of double consciousness. Proceedings of the Society for Psychical Research 7, 221-58.

Hofstadter, D.R. and Dennett, D.C. (eds) (1981) The Mind's I: Fantasies and Reflections on Self and Soul. London, Penguin.

Holland, J. (ed.) (2001) Ecstasy: The Complete Guide: A Comprehensive Look at the Risks and Benefits of MDMA. Rochester, VT, Park Street Press.

Holmes, D.S. (1987) The influence of meditation versus rest on physiological arousal. In M. West (ed.) The Psychology of Meditation. Oxford, Clarendon Press, 81-103.

Holmstrom, David. 1992, Christian Science Monitor

Holt, J. (1999) Blindsight in debates about qualia. Journal of Consciousness Studies 6(5), 54-71.

Holloway RL (1996) Evolution of the human brain. In: Lock A, Peters CR (eds) Handbook of human symbolic evolution. Oxford University Press, Oxford

Iacoboni M, Woods RP, Brass M, Bekkering H, Mazziotta JC, Rizzolatti G (1999) Cortical mechanisms of human imitation. Science 286: 2526–2528.

Iacoboni M, Koski LM, Brass M, Bekkering H, Woods RP, Dubeau MC, Mazziotta JC, Rizzolatti G (2001) Reafferent copies of imitated actions in the right superior temporal cortex. Proc Natl Acad Sci USA 98: 13995–13999.

Jeannerod M (1988) The neural and behavioural organization of goal-directed movements. Clarendon Press, Oxford.

Johnson-Frey SH, Maloof FR, Newman-Norlund R, Farrer C, Inati S, Grafton ST (2003) Actions or hand-objects interactions? Human inferior frontal cortex and action observation. Neuron 39: 1053–1058.

Jackson, F. (1982) Epiphenomenal qualia. Philosophical Quarterly 32, 127-36.

James, W. (1890) The Principles of Psychology (2 volumes). London, Macmillan.

James, W. (1902) The Varieties of Religious Experience: A Study in Human Nature. New York and London, Longmans, Green and Co.

Jansen, K. (2001) Ketamine: Dreams and Realities. Sarasota, FL, Multidisciplinary Association for Psychedelic Studies.

Jay, M. (ed.) (1999) Artificial Paradises: A Drugs Reader. London, Penguin.

Jaynes, J. (1976) The Origin of Consciousness in the Breakdown of the Bicameral Mind. New York, Houghton Mifflin.

Johnson, M.K. and Raye, C.L. (1981) Reality monitoring. Psychological Review 88, 67-85.

Kadim I, Mahgoub O, Baqir S et al. (2015) Cultured meat from muscle stem cells: a review of challenges and prospects. J Integr Agr 14: 222–233

Kandel, E. R. In Search of Memory: The Emergence of a New Science of Mind, W. W. Norton & Company (2007).

Kandel E. R. Schwartz JH, Jessel TM. Principles of neural sciences. New York; McGraw Hill, 2000.

Kanwisher, N. (2001) Neural events and perceptual awareness. Cognition

79, 89-113; also reprinted inS. Dehaene (ed.) The Cognitive Neuroscience of Consciousness. Cambridge, MA, MIT Press, 89-113.

Karn, K. and Hayhoe, M. (2000) Memory representations guide targeting eye movements in a natural task. Visual Cognition 7, 673-703.

Kennedy, H., & Dehay, C. (1988). Functional implications of the anatomical organization of the callosal projections of visual areas V1 and V2 in the macaque monkey. Behav. Brain Res., 29, 225–236.

Kentridge, R.W. and Heywood, C.A. (1999) The status of blindsight. Journal of Consciousness Studies 6(5), 3-11.

Kihlstrom, J.F. (1996) Perception without awareness of what is perceived, learning without awareness of what is learned. In M. Velmans (ed.) The Science of Consciousness. London, Routledge, 23-46.

Kosslyn, S.M. (1980) Image and Mind. Cambridge, MA, Harvard University Press.

Kosslyn, S.M. (1988) Aspects of a cognitive neuroscience of mental imagery. Science 240, 1621-6.

Kinsbourne, M. (1995), 'The intralaminar thalamic nucleii', Consciousness and Cognition, 4.

Kjaer, Troels, Camilla Bertelsen, Paola Piccini, David Brooks, Jorgen Alving, and Hans Lou. "Increased Dopamine Tone during Meditation- Induced Change of Consciousness." Cognitive Brain Research 13, no. 2 (April 2002)

Kölmel HW. 1985. Complex visual hallucinations in the hemianopic field. J Neurol Neurosurg Psychiatry.

Koenig, Harold. "Research on Religion, Spirituality, and Mental Health: A Review." Canadian Journal of Psychiatry 54, no. 5 (May 2009)

Koenig, Harold, ed. Handbook of Religion and Mental Health. San Diego, CA: Academic Press, 1998

Kraepelin E. Psychiatry: A Textbook for Students and Physicians. New York, NY: Science History Publications; 1990.

Lauglin, Charles, John McManus, and Eugene d'Aquili. Brain, Symbol, and Experience. 2nd ed. New York: Columbia University Press, 1992

Lakoff, G. and M. Johnson (1999). Philosophy in the flesh. Basic Books: New York.

LeDoux, J. E. (1996). The emotional brain. New York: Simon & Schuster.

LeDoux, J.E. (1992), 'Emotion and the amygdala', in The Amygdala: Neurobiological Aspects of Emo- tion, Memory and Mental Dysfunction, ed J.P. Aggleton (New York: Wiley-Liss).

Levin, D.T. and Simons, D.J. (1997) Failure to detect changes to attended objects in motion pictures. Psychonomic Bulletin and Review 4, 501-6.

Levine,J. (1983) Materialism and qualia: the explanatory gap. Pacific Philosophical Quarterly 64, 354-61.

Levine,J. (2001) Purple Haze: The Puzzle of Consciousness. New York, Oxford University Press. Levine, S. (1979) A Gradual Awakening. New York, Doubleday.

Levinson, B.W. (1965) States of awareness during general anaesthesia. British Journal of Anaesthesia 37, 544-6.

Lewicki, P., Czyzewska, M. and Hoffman, H. (1987) Unconscious acquisition of complex procedural knowledge. Journal of Experimental Psychology: Learning, Memory and Cognition 13, 523-30.

Lewicki, P., Hill, T. and Bizot, E. (1988) Acquisition of procedural knowledge about a pattern of stimuli that cannot be articulated. Cognitive Psychology 20, 24-37.

Lewicki, P., Hill, T. and Czyzewska, M. (1992) Nonconscious acquisition of information. American Psychologist 47, 796-801.

Manthey S, Schubotz RI, von Cramon DY (2003). Premotor cortex in observing erroneous action: an fMRI study. Brain Res Cogn Brain Res 15: 296–307.

Mesulam MM, Mufson EJ (1982) Insula of the old world monkey. III: Efferent cortical output and comments on function. J Comp Neurol 212: 38–52.

Naskar, Abhijit. "Homo: A Brief History of Consciousness", 2015

Naskar, Abhijit. "What is Mind?", 2016

Naskar, Abhijit. "Love, God & Neurons: Memoir of A Scientist who found himself by getting lost", 2016

Naskar, Abhijit. "Principia Humanitas", 2017

Naskar, Abhijit. "We Are All Black: A Treatise on Racism", 2017

Naskar, Abhijit. "Either Civilized or Phobic: A Treatise on Homosexuality", 2017

Naskar, Abhijit. "I Am The Thread: My Mission", 2017

Naskar, Abhijit. "The Bengal Tigress: A Treatise on Gender Equality", 2017

Naskar, Abhijit. "Morality Absolute", 2017

Naskar, Abhijit. "Build Bridges not Walls: In the name of Americana", 2018

Naskar, Abhijit. "Fabric of Humanity", 2018

Naskar, Abhijit. "Lives To Serve Before I Sleep", 2019

Naskar, Abhijit. "Citizens of Peace: Beyond the Savagery of Sovereignty", 2019

Naskar, Abhijit. "The Constitution of The United Peoples of Earth", 2019

Naskar, Abhijit. "Neurons Giveth, Neurons Taketh Away | Abhijit Naskar | TEDxIIMRanchi", 2019 https://www.youtube.com/watch?v=B NX-Q0ySm80

Naskar, Abhijit. "Mission Reality", 2019

Naskar, Abhijit. "Operation Justice: To Make A Society That Needs No Law", 2019

Naskar, Abhijit. "Every Generation Needs Caretakers: The Gospel of Patriotism", 2020

Naskar, Abhijit. "Hurricane Humans: Give me accountability, I'll give you peace", 2020

Naskar, Abhijit. "Revolution Indomable", 2020

Naskar, Abhijit. "Servitude is Sanctitude", 2020

Naskar, Abhijit. "Good Scientist: When Science and Service Combine", 2020

Newberg, Andrew, and Jeremy Iversen. "The Neural Basis of the Complex Mental Task of Meditation: Neurotransmitter and Neurochemical Considerations." Medical Hypotheses 61, no. 2 (2003).

Newberg, Andrew. "How God Changes Your Brain: An Introduction to Jewish Neurotheology", CCAR Journal: The Reform Jewish Quarterly, Winter 2016.

Newberg, Andrew, and Stephanie Newberg. "A Neuropsychological

Perspective on Spiritual Development." In Handbook of Spiritual Development in Childhood and Adolescence, edited by Eugene Roehlkepartain, Pamela King, Linda Wagener, and Peter Benson. London: Sage Publications, Inc., 2005

Newberg, Andrew. "The Neurotheology Link An Intersection Between Spirituality and Health", Alternative and Complimentary Therapies, Vol 21 No 1, February 2015.

Newberg, Andrew, Nancy Wintering, Dharma Khalsa, Hannah Roggenkamp, and Mark Waldman. "Meditation Effects on Cognitive Function and Cerebral Blood Flow in Subjects with Memory Loss: A Preliminary Study." Journal of Alzheimer's Disease 20, no. 2 (2010)

Nash, M. (1995), 'Glimpses of the mind', Time.

Nesse RM. Proximate and evolutionary studies of anxiety, stress and depression: synergy at the interface. Neurosci Biobehav Rev. 1999;23:895-903.

Nicolelis, Miguel. (2011) "Beyond Boundaries: The New Neuroscience of Connecting Brains with Machines--- and How It Will Change Our Lives", Times Books

O'Hara, K. and Scutt, T. (1996) There is no hard problem of consciousness. Journal of Consciousness Studies 3(4), 290-302, reprinted in J. Shear (ed.) (1997) Explaining Consciousness. Cambridge, MA, MIT Press, 69-82.

O'Regan, J.K. (1992) Solving the "real" mysteries of visual perception: the world as an outside memory. Canadian Journal of Psychology 46, 461-88.

O'Regan, J.K. and Noe, A. (2001) A sensorimotor account of vision and visual consciousness. Behavioral and Brain Sciences 24(5), 883-917.

O'Regan, J.K., Rensink, R.A. and Clark,].]. (1999) Change-blindness as a result of "mudsplashes." Nature 398, 34.

Ornstein, R.E. (1977) The Psychology of Consciousness (2nd edn). New York, Harcourt.

Ornstein, R.E. (1986) The Psychology of Consciousness (3rd edn). New York, Pehguin.

Ornstein, R.E. (1992) The Evolution of Consciousness. New York, Touchstone.

Penfield W, Faulk ME (1955) The insula: further observations on its function. Brain 78: 445– 470.

Penrose, R. (1994), Shadows of the Mind (Oxford: Oxford University Press).

Penrose, R. (1989), The Emperor's New Mind: Concerning Computers, Minds and The Laws of Physics (Oxford: Oxford University Press).

Persinger, "'I would kill in God's name' role of sex, weekly church attendance, report of a religious experience and limbic lability" Perceptual and Motor Skills 1997.

Persinger "Experimental simulation of the God experience" Neurotheology 2003.

Persinger, M. A. (1993b). Personality changes following brain injury as a grief response to the loss of sense of self: Phenomenological themes as indices of local lability and neurocognitive restructuring as psycho- therapy. Psychological Reports, 72

Persinger, Corradini, Clement, Keaney, et al "Neurotheology and its convergence with neuroquantology" NeuroQuantology 2010.

Persinger, Koren and St-Pierre "The electromagnetic induction of mystical and altered states within the laboratory" Journal of Consciousness Exploration and Research 2010.

Persinger "Case report: A prototypical spontaneous 'sensed presence' of a sentient being and concomitant electroencephalographic activity in the clinical laboratory" Neurocase 2008.

Persinger and Saroka "Potential production of Hughlings Jackson's "parasitic consciousness" by physiologically-patterned weak transcerebral magnetic fields: QEEG and source localization" Epilepsy & Behavior 28 (2013).

Persinger. "The neuropsychiatry of paranormal experiences". J Neuropsychiatry Clin Neurosci 2001.

Persinger. "Neuropsychological bases of god beliefs", New York: Praeger, 1987

Persinger. "Temporal lobe epileptic signs and correlative behaviors displayed by normal populations", Journal of General Psychology, 1986

Perry BD, Pollard R. Homeostasis, stress, trauma, and adaptation. A neurodevelopmental view of childhood trauma. Child Adolesc Psychiatr Clin N Am. 1998;7:33.

Paré, D. & Llinás, R. (1995), 'Conscious and preconscious processes as seen from the standpoint of sleep-waking cycle neurophysiology', Neuropsychologia, 33.

Phillips ML, Young AW, Senior C, Brammer M, Andrew C, Calder AJ, Bullmore ET, Perrett DI, Rowland D, Williams SC, Gray JA, David AS (1997) A specific neural substrate for perceiving facial expressions of disgust. Nature 389: 495–498.

Phillips ML, Young AW, Scott SK, Calder AJ, Andrew C, Giampietro V, Williams SC, Bullmore ET, Brammer M, Gray JA (1998) Neural responses to facial and vocal expressions of fear and disgust. Proc R Soc Lond B Biol Sci 265: 1809–1817.

Puce A, Perrett D (2003) Electrophysiological and brain imaging of biological motion. Philosoph Trans Royal Soc Lond, Series B, 358: 435–445.

Ramachandran VS. Behavioral and magnetoencephalographic correlates of plasticity in the adult human brain. Proc Natl Acad Sci USA 1993; 90: 10413–20.

Ramachandran VS. Phantom limbs, neglect syndromes, repressed memories, and Freudian psychology. Int Rev Neurobiol 1994; 37: 291–333.

Ramachandran VS. Plasticity and functional recovery in neurology. Clin Med 2005; 5: 368–73.

Ramachandran VS, Hirstein W. The perception of phantom limbs. The D. O. Hebb lecture. Brain 1998; 121: 1603–30.

Ramachandran VS, Rogers-Ramachandran D, Cobb S. Touching the phantom limb. Nature 1995; 377: 489–90.

Ramachandran VS, Rogers-Ramachandran D. Phantom limbs and neural plasticity. Arch Neurol 2000; 57: 317–20.

Ramachandran VS, Rogers-Ramachandran D. It's all done with mirrors. Sci Am Mind 2007; 18: 16–9.

Ramachandran VS, Rogers-Ramachandran D. Sensations referred to a patient's phantom arm from another subjects intact arm: perceptual correlates of mirror neurons. Med Hypotheses 2008; 70: 1233–4.

Ramachandran VS, Rogers-Ramachandran D, Stewart M. Perceptual correlates of massive cortical reorganization. Science 1992; 258: 1159–60.

Rizzolatti G, Craighero L (2004) The mirror-neuron system. Annu Rev Neurosci 27: 169–192.

Rizzolatti G, Fogassi L, Gallese V (2001) Neurophysiological mechanisms underlying the understanding and imitation of action. Nature Rev Neurosci 2:661–670.

Rock I, Victor J. Vision and touch: an experimentally created conflict between the two senses. Science 1964; 143: 594–6.

Rose´n B, Lundborg G. Training with a mirror in rehabilitation of the hand. Scand J Plast Reconstr Surg Hand Surg 2005; 39: 104–8.

Roberts, TA; Smalley, J; Ahrendt, D (December 2020). "Effect of gender affirming hormones on athletic performance in transwomen and transmen: implications for sporting organisations and legislators". British Journal of Sports Medicine. 55 (11): 577–583

Royet JP, Plailly J, Delon-Martin C, Kareken DA, Segebarth C (2003) fMRI of emotional responses to odors: influence of hedonic valence and judgment, handedness, and gender. Neuroimage 20: 713–728.

Rozin R Haidt J and McCauley CR (2000) Disgust. In: Lewis M, Haviland-Jones JM (eds) Handbook of Emotion. 2nd Edition. Guilford Press, New York, pp 637–653.

Saxe R, Carey S, Kanwisher N (2004) Understanding other minds: linking developmental psychology and functional neuroimaging. Annu Rev Psychol 55: 87–124.

S. J. Russell and P. Norvig, Artificial intelligence: a modern approach (3rd edition): Prentice Hall, 2009.

Singer T, Seymour B, O'Doherty J, Kaube H, Dolan RJ, Frith CD (2004) Empathy for pain involves the affective but not the sensory components of pain. Science 303: 1157–1162.

Smith A (1759) The theory of moral sentiments (ed. 1976). Clarendon Press, Oxford.

Sprengelmeyer R, Rausch M, Eysel UT, Przuntek H (1998) Neural structures associated with recognition of facial expressions of basic emotions Proc R Soc Lond B Biol Sci 265: 1927–1931.

Strafella AP, Paus T (2000) Modulation of cortical excitability during action observation: a transcranial magnetic stimulation study. NeuroReport 11: 2289–2292.

Schilling, Vincent. 2017, indian country today

Stein, Stephen K. 2017, The Sea in World History: Exploration, Travel, and Trade

Simonsen R (2015) Eating for the future: veganism and the challenge of in vitro meat. In: Stapleton P, Byers A (Hg). Biopolitics and utopia. Palgrave Macmillan, New York (2015), S 167–190

Tanaka K (1996) Inferotemporal cortex and object vision. Ann Rev Neurosci. 19: 109–140.

Tesla N. "My Inventions", 1919

T. R. Society, "Machine learning: the power and promise of computers that learn by example," ed. The Royal Society, 2017.

Tomasello M, Call J (1997) Primate cognition. Oxford University Press, Oxford.

Tremblay C, Robert M, Pascual-Leone A, Lepore F, Nguyen DK, Carmant L, Bouthillier A, Theoret H (2004) Action observation and execution: intracranial recordings in a human subject. Neurology. 63: 937–938.

Umilta MA, Kohler E, Gallese V, Fogassi L, Fadiga L, Keysers C, Rizzolatti G (2001) "I know what you are doing": a neurophysiological study. Neuron 32: 91–101.

Wiik, Anna; Lundberg, Tommy R; Rullman, Eric; Andersson, Daniel P; Holmberg, Mats; Mandić, Mirko; Brismar, Torkel B; Dahlqvist Leinhard, Olof; Chanpen, Setareh; Flanagan, John N; Arver, Stefan; Gustafsson, Thomas (1 March 2020). "Muscle Strength, Size, and Composition Following 12 Months of Gender-affirming Treatment in Transgender Individuals". The Journal of Clinical Endocrinology & Metabolism. 105 (3): e805–e813.

Made in the USA
Middletown, DE
22 March 2022